What they're saying about
DR. BISCOTTI & THE HUMAN CONDITION

"Lisa Soland's *Dr. Biscotti and the Human Condition* is a
tour de force and a masterpiece. Its theme centers on
nothing less than life's reasons and randomness. Characters
represent the fourth dimension—time rather than space. By
the end of the play, we learn how life can differ for an array
of people, all linked by the interlocutor—their therapist,
Dr. Biscotti. This play is original, entertaining, at times
shocking, and brilliantly crafted. Dramatically, it has
surprises and a wonderful build to a shocking conclusion. I
could not get it, or the deep philosophical and sociological
issues, out of my head for weeks after seeing it. I am a long-
time fan of Ms. Soland, but this is perhaps her deepest play.
I would love to see it get all the attention it deserves."
– *Andrew Bonime, Feature Film Producer/Composer*

"I greatly enjoyed and admired *Dr. Biscotti and the Human
Condition*. Playwright Lisa Soland has such a great ability
to make credible, rounded, and lovable characters. They
are flawed as human beings, which means we can relate to
them, but we also have quite complex feelings toward them.
This gives a fantastic emotional texture to the piece
(and to all her writing)."
– *Kieron Barry, Reviewer for the Metro Pulse*

"Absolutely riveting dialogue and characters. *Dr. Biscotti* is
an excellent work. I was absolutely captured by the
characters and their stories."
– *Steven L. Sears, TV Producer/Writer*

(Rustin Comer designed the set for the West Coast premiere. The actors in the photo are: Michelle DeLynn as Sherie, Paul Cuneo as Steve, Todd Covert as Dr. Biscotti, and Theodora Greece as Abbey. Photo by Steven L. Sears.)

DR. BISCOTTI
and the
HUMAN CONDITION

By Lisa Soland

All Original
Play Publishing

DR. BISCOTTI & THE HUMAN CONDITION
Written by Lisa Soland
Copyright © 2008 by Lisa Soland

Published in 2024 by All Original Play Publishing
P.O. Box 32381
Knoxville, TN 37930
AllOriginalPlays@gmail.com

First Edition: April 2024
Printed in the United States of America
Graphic Design by All Original Play Publishing
Photography by Steven L. Sears
        (Back cover photo of Theodora Greece as *Abbey*.)

ISBN: 978-1-956218-34-3
Library of Congress Control Number: 2024904598

This play is dedicated to Brian Matthews for his love for humanity, true empathy, and willingness to place the well-being of another person ahead of his own.

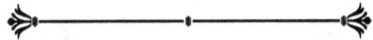

CHARACTERS

DR. BISCOTTI: A psychologist, 45 to 55 years old.

ABBEY: A young woman in her 20s, withdrawn.

STEVE: A man in his late 20s with an undercurrent of anger.

SHERIE: A woman about to turn 40, beautiful.

GEORGE: A man of any age, possibly 30s, about to be married. Experiencing the happiest time of his life.

PLACE

Dr. Biscotti's office.

TIME

ACT ONE

DR. BISCOTTI AND THE HUMAN CONDITION received its West Coast premiere at Theatre Encino in Los Angeles, California, on October 17, 2009. It was produced by Melanie Ewbank, directed by Lisa Soland, and the assistant director/stage manager was Vincent Archer. The set design was by Rustin Comer. The cast was as follows:

DR. BISCOTTI .... Todd Covert
ABBEY ....Theodora Greece
STEVE .... Paul Cuneo
SHERIE .... Michelle DeLynn
GEORGE .... Scott Ford

DR. BISCOTTI AND THE HUMAN CONDITION was subsequently produced by Theater23, with Tom Eubanks as Founding Artistic Director, and directed by Lisa Soland at the Knoxville Convention Center, Knoxville, Tennessee, opening September 20, 2024.

A staged reading of the play was presented at Pellissippi State College in Knoxville, Tennessee, on September 6, 2009, directed by Charles R. Miller. *Dr. Biscotti* was played by Greg Congleton, *Steve* by James Francis, and *Sherie* by Susannah Devereux.

DESCRIPTION

Dr. Biscotti and the Human Condition takes place in the office of a psychologist as he relives the story of a recent, tragic event. Throughout the play, we witness how choice and happenstance uniquely impact the course of his clients' lives.

————————————————————

This is a full-length play with adult language, requiring 3 males and two females.

3 m, 2 f

"The fault, dear Brutus, is not in our stars,
But in ourselves, that we are underlings."

– *Shakespeare's Julius Caesar, Cassius to Brutus*

DR. BISCOTTI &
THE HUMAN CONDITION

ACT ONE

Scene 1

SETTING: *We are in the office of psychologist DR.*
BISCOTTI, which consists of five
platforms, his being the largest. A
rudimentary desk and chair sit center
stage on his platform. There are two
smaller platforms on either side of his,
all containing matching chairs of their
own. Attached to and behind each of
the five platforms is a wall, but only on
the back, not on the sides. On the sides,
there is nothing but air and a bit of
space dividing them from each other,
but more importantly, from DR.
BISCOTTI'S. The chairs are all the
same—padded, elegant and
comfortable. Each of the four smaller
platforms contains a clock that hangs
on the upstage wall. Each clock tells a
different time. Reading from stage
right to left—11:00, 10:00, 9:00, and
12:00. The clocks do not change time.
They remain the same throughout the

> *entire play. On Dr. Biscotti's desk sits a desk lamp, a desk clock, an appointment book, a pot of hot coffee, two coffee cups, and a plate of biscotti.*

AT RISE:　　*It is Thursday at 9:00 am. A light comes up softly on Dr. Biscotti's platform, where we find him sitting on the front edge of his desk, motionless. Now in silhouette, we see DR. BISCOTTI reach over and turn on his desk lamp, which casts a bit of green light onto the plate of biscotti. DR. BISCOTTI remains motionless, his eyes softly focused on the plate.*

DR. BISCOTTI: *(Voice over.)* The Italians use the term biscotti to refer to any type of cookie. We Americans use the word to describe a long, dry, twice-baked cookie with a rounded top and a flat bottom made especially for dipping into coffee or wine.
(Beat.)
The dough is shaped into a 12-inch log and baked until firm. After it cools, the log is cut into diagonal slices and baked again to draw out the moisture, thus producing a crisp, hard, textured cookie.
(Beat.)

Though there are many varieties and flavors, the consistency of biscotti remains the same—dry and hard, thus giving it a...very long shelf life.

(Lights come up full on center stage. DR. BISCOTTI is dipping biscotti into his cup of coffee.)

DR. BISCOTTI: *(Somewhat to the audience.)*
I dip biscotti into coffee, not wine because I enjoy eating it while I work. The coffee stimulates my thoughts, and the sweet of the cookie, well, the sweet of the cookie, is just that—sweet.
(Lights down on DR. BISCOTTI and up on ABBEY, who sits on her platform just to his left)
ABBEY: *(She is talking to DR. BISCOTTI, but not directly, as if he were out over the audience.)*
She's got these lumps. They're kind of squishy and moveable. The first one I found was on her back—about midway down. Obvious. But it's not the biggest. The biggest is on her chest. I wouldn't have found that one except for the fact that she loves to be scratched there, and one day, I itched it—the lump. So, I thought I'd take her in. Today. 10:30. She's in the car.
(She rises and crosses to an imaginary window downstage.)
I parked under the shade, so I'm sure she's fine. The last couple of days, she hasn't been eating much, about a third of the usual. I coax her on, sitting with her because I notice if I sit with her,

she does better. She eats more. Anyway, she's in the car, so if my mind wanders, it's because part of me is with her. Out there. In the car.

(ABBEY sits.)

I've had her nine years now. We're not sure how old she was when I brought her home. Some guy left her in the apartment when he moved out. Just left her, no food, no water. She was around six maybe, the vet said. So...15, maybe now. Pretty old, I guess, for a dog. Wish I'd found her earlier in her life. Earlier in mine. It just goes by, either way, doesn't it? Time. It just goes by.

(Beat.)

She never got over the abuse. Not really. I finally accepted the fact that she wouldn't, no matter how hard I tried to love it out of her. She had her own pace with it—the speed at which she healed. Still, to this day, when I fold laundry... Well, instead of running out of the room like she used to, she just looks at me suspiciously. I have never, ever hit her, but she still thinks I could. One day, I might just up and change my mind about it all and smack her one. Breaks my heart, really.

STEVE: *(Lights come up full on STEVE, who is on the downstage platform, just to DR. BISCOTTI'S right. He too is addressing DR. BISCOTTI, but not directly, as if he were out over the audience.)*

I would have never had to have anything to do with the man ever again. But, my grandmother died, and next thing you know, we're planning a

funeral. And when funerals come in a family,
you've got to arrange things...and you've got to do
things you normally would never, ever do. Like...
call your father. The guy's a prick. Really. A
f-ing prick.

ABBEY: I like being with her because there's no
pressure. Pressure to be happy. I hate that. It's
exhausting, really. And I don't care who you're
with, it's there. "Come on, now! Be happy. Be
chipper." It's exhausting. Rose just lets me be
who I am. I don't have to adjust myself.
(Beat.)
It's all a game, really. A game of who's got it more
together. Who's happiest. Every time I finish
visiting with somebody, I have to go home to rest
and wash it off. The lies. The lying. "I'm this great
person who's always feeling great." I gotta wash
that off my skin. So, I take a bath. And then I go
to bed.

SHERIE: *(Lights up on SHERIE, who is on the platform
far stage right, talking to DR. BISCOTTI out
over the audience.)*
I'm going to be 40 this Tuesday. Forty. You know
what happens to a woman when she turns 40?
She shrivels up like the Wicked Witch of the West
and shrinks into the ground. Well, that's how
society treats her, whether you like it or not. Like
she's nothing. Nothing.
(Boldly.)
And I am not nothing.
(Beat.)

Am I?

STEVE: When I heard my dad's voice on the phone, I thought I would throw up.

(STEVE stands and crosses downstage.)

So I carried the phone into the bathroom and talked to him there...standing next to the toilet. I just stood there next to the toilet, in front of the mirror, searching my face, wondering which parts of me were like him. While I listened to him on the phone—stall and stutter.

SHERIE: *(She stands and crosses downstage.)*

I look in the mirror almost daily now. The lines. The ever-expanding lines. I read somewhere that a person has the face God gave them from birth to 40, but after 40, they have the face they gave themselves. You know what I have to say about that? What kind of God would have created wrinkles in the first place?!

(Beat.)

I tell my husband, I want to have some work done, you know? Some Botox injections here and there, and he says no. Just like that. He rarely says no about anything. Like he knows something I don't. Like he thinks the wrinkles are going to serve some sort of purpose, expanding all over my face.

(Begging.)

"Please. Pretty please. Just a little Botox," I say. He says, "No. We're downsizing." I said, "Yes, exactly. And I'd like to start with my wrinkles."

STEVE: He's in his fifties now. Probably all shriveled up.
　　　　The ol' prick. I was only nine when he left.
　　　　Second to the oldest. Can you imagine that?
　　　　Leaving four kids? My mother was pregnant with
　　　　the youngest—John. She never told us anything.
　　　　So we made up our own reasons why. But there
　　　　really is no reason, is there? I mean, what kind of
　　　　a reason can you have for walking out one night,
　　　　just up and walking out? One minute, the family
　　　　is eating dinner, and we're out of milk, and the
　　　　next minute, it's 20 years later, and you're
　　　　planning a funeral.
ABBEY: It just goes by, either way, doesn't it? Time. It
　　　　just goes by.
STEVE: What was he afraid of? Four kids and a wife? I
　　　　can think of a lot worse things to be afraid of.
SHERIE: Wrinkles.
STEVE: Like four kids and a wife, 20 years later.
　　　　(He sits.)
　　　　We were very well-behaved. Very well. Too well,
　　　　maybe. Kept it all in. Somehow, I got elected to
　　　　make the call. I had "more control," they said—
　　　　"The least angry among us." Well, what do you
　　　　know about that?—"the least angry." The vote
　　　　was three to one, so I made the call to the prick.
　　　　(STEVE rises and crosses downstage.)
　　　　In the bathroom, next to the toilet.
DR. BISCOTTI: *(Addresses the audience.)*
　　　　There are a series of biological events that are
　　　　common to most humans, some of which are
　　　　inevitable—like death, for instance. The manner

in which humans react to or cope with these common biological events is often times referred to as "the human condition."

SHERIE: *(She rises.)* So I was standing there in the bathroom, day before yesterday, and what do you think I find? Not a longer wrinkle, not another gray hair, but...a lump in my breast. A lump. Well, that changes everything, doesn't it?

ABBEY: It's big, the one on her chest. Scared me when I found it.

SHERIE: I'm embarrassed to talk about it because I don't want people thinking that I was, you know, feeling myself up. Some old lady turning 40, feeling herself up.

ABBEY: *(With great difficulty.)* I just can't keep from thinking that... Well, she's old. She's an old, very sweet dog. My sweet, Rose. I figure maybe sometime in the next...I don't know...six months or so... So, I'm thinking I need to start adjusting to the idea that someday I'm going to have to go through the process of losing her.

DR. BISCOTTI: *(He sits on the front edge of his desk, to audience.)*
Yet understanding the precise nature and scope of what is meant by the "human condition" is itself a philosophical problem because the term has also been used to describe joy and other elevated feelings or emotions associated with human existence.

GEORGE: *(Lights come up on the last playing area, far stage left, where we find GEORGE standing. He also talks to DR. BISCOTTI as if he is out over the audience. GEORGE is exuberantly happy while revealing the news of a lifetime.)*

Hey, Doc. Sorry, I'm late. Well, I popped the question, and she said YES! Spent the entire morning in bed, celebrating. I made her breakfast first—eggs, bacon, fried potatoes and then she made me pancakes. Pancakes! I gotta tell you, this is going to be great. You probably wondered what happened to me, didn't you? Well, it's hard to disrupt a fellow when he's in heaven and I got you to thank for it, Doc. Thank you. I can't thank you enough. Thank you, thank you, thank you.

(Beat.)

Oh, I know, "You didn't do it," but you helped me do it. Whatever it was I did, and I'm grateful.

(Beat.)

You should have seen her face when I asked her. It was like, surprised but not really surprised. Just the way a face should look when you ask it to spend the rest of its life with you. The most beautiful face I've ever seen, just looking at me, saying yes over and over and over again—YES! Ah, it was great! Absolutely great!

(He sits.)

I don't really know what to talk about today. It seems like I don't have anything more to say. I mean, what can a person say except...MAN, CAN SHE MAKE PANCAKES! Holy cow. Not the box kind. Oh no. These got flour in 'em. Real flour. And sugar, vanilla, I don't know what else, but not nothing from a box. The kitchen was a mess. An absolute mess.

ABBEY: I guess I'm a little concerned with what I'll do. I mean, nine years, and she's pretty much my best friend, you know.

GEORGE: "George, why don't you marry your best friend?" Brilliant, Doc. I don't know why I didn't think of that.

ABBEY: I take her with me, places. Everywhere, really.

GEORGE: Solved all my problems.

ABBEY: A couple nights ago, I had this really weird dream. It wasn't really a dream. Well, part of it was.

GEORGE: All my dreams are finally coming true, Doc. I got a life. What can I say? I finally got a life with meaning.

ABBEY: I'm not really sure what it means.
(Beat.)
I was asleep, sleeping. And I was having some ordinary dream. But while I was dreaming, some other part of me was aware of the bedroom. I became frightened because a tall, dark figure, ominous really, entered and moved; I can't really say it walked, but it moved right up next to me on the bed while I was sleeping and laid its hands, black hands, down on my chest. I was terrified.
(Beat.)
Right then, Rose, who was sleeping next to the bed, growled menacingly, and I woke up with this terror embedded in my chest, and it wouldn't go away. And now I'm feeling afraid of the dark, so I

turn on the bathroom light and leave the door open just enough to cast as much light as I need to see every inch and cranny of my bedroom. It wasn't enough, though, so I go on a search to find my Bible, which was buried in the closet under years of tax returns. But I found it. Blew off the dust and got back into bed. I didn't read it or anything. I just laid it on my chest so I could go back to sleep. And I did, surprisingly. Fell right back to sleep. But it was Rose who growled and woke me up. You see? She's sensitive to that sort of thing. She's been my protector. All this time, she's kept me from trouble. Not that I could explain to you the dark figure, but I'm telling you, on some level, it was real. And I've been sleeping with that Bible on my chest every night since.

GEORGE: I'll be sleeping next to her for the rest of my life.

ABBEY: But she woke me up with her growl, and I can't even imagine what it would be like not having her there, sleeping beside me.

SHERIE: I haven't been able to sleep since. Waiting to find out for sure what it was. I went to the O.B.G.Y.N., and that same day, they sent me to the surgeon, who clears out his schedule for me. He pokes some needle in the breast to see what sort of fluid is in there, you know? Good or bad. And nothing suspicious shows up, but still, the surgeon is all worried. He says I could just sort of blow it off, or we could have it removed, only then will we know for sure. My husband asks him, "If she were your wife, what would you do?" And he says, "I'd remove it. And I'd do it as fast as I could." And I'm thinking, isn't anyone going to ask me what I want to do? Isn't anyone going to ask me?

GEORGE: I asked her, and she said yes. I stuttered a bit 'cause I was nervous as all get out.

STEVE: So as he's stuttering away, I just interrupted him and said, "Listen, Dad, I'm calling because grandma's dying. Your mother. She's dying, and we were all thinking you might want to know."

ABBEY: I don't really want to know. She's in the car, and we're going to the vet, but part of me really doesn't want to know what the lumps are. They could be benign.
(Hopefully.)
They could.

SHERIE: *(She sits.)* I explained to these two gentlemen that I drink a lot of caffeine and that lumpy breasts run in my family, but they both just stood there looking at me, sitting there with this hideous paper towel thing hanging over one of my shoulders. Ugh. I hate this. No more bathing suit shots, no more magazine covers. Not like I ever did a Sports Illustrated, but I've done covers. Well, one. One cover. I was on the cover of Glamour when I was sixteen, but...oh hell. Screw it. I'm the Wicked Witch of the West, and I'm shriveling.

STEVE: So, he's on the other line all shriveled up, and I say, "Dad, are you there?" He says yeah, all weak-like. And part of me is starting to feel sorry for the guy. Explain that. Sorry for the prick. And then he says, "Well, that's life." Just like that, "That's life." Like he's some sort of specialist on the subject.

(He sits.)

SHERIE: Do you know what it's like to have a goal, a dream, and then not be able to make that happen? Do you know what that's like? And this is something I have no control of, this...growing old. I didn't ask for this. I mean, like, what am I going to do now, huh? What?

STEVE: My dad—the great philosopher.

SHERIE: I had a purpose.

ABBEY: After that dream, it got me thinking.

(She rises, with poignancy.)

Maybe there is some sort of dark force, you know. Wandering around, trying to get us all to stumble. To fall.

SHERIE: I had a purpose, and now my life is just some sort of pile of rubble lying on the floor.

STEVE: The great shriveled-up philosopher.

ABBEY: And maybe this dark force would like it if I just stayed in bed all day and didn't go out and took a lot of baths and avoided seeing people. Maybe it would enjoy me...giving up.

STEVE: Why is it that guys like him thrive and nice little old ladies like my grandma have to die? Why?

SHERIE: Why? Why me?

DR. BISCOTTI: *(Rises and crosses downstage, to audience.)*

All primates are aware of the passing of time. All primates can remember the past and imagine the future, and all are somewhat aware of their own mortality. But it is only human primates, human beings, who ask themselves—"What is the meaning of life? Why was I born? Why am I here? Where will I go when I die?" They come to me for answers, not like I can give them any, but I listen. I listen.

ABBEY: Maybe this dark...thing would like it if I thought life had no meaning at all.
(She sits.)

DR. BISCOTTI: *(He returns to his desk and sits again on the downstage edge of the desk.)*
Some of my clients don't even know my real name. They don't pay attention. They're too involved, really, in their own lives. But every once in a while, someone peeks through the shadowed veil of their existence and finds me...sipping.
(He sips his coffee.)

GEORGE: *(For the first time, GEORGE turns and talks directly to DR. BISCOTTI.)*
So what do you think, Doc? Is it time for me to go, or should we just keep on like this?

DR. BISCOTTI: *(To GEORGE.)* It's time for you to go, George.

GEORGE: *(Genuinely surprised.)* Really?

DR. BISCOTTI: Yes, really.

GEORGE: Won't you miss me?

DR. BISCOTTI: What do you think?

GEORGE: Yes, I think you will. I think you'll miss me terribly, Doc. But I think you'll eventually get over it.

DR. BISCOTTI: Eventually.

GEORGE: *(He rises, sincerely.)* Doc, this has meant...a lot to me. What can I say? I'll drop by the last payment next week. So...well.

DR. BISCOTTI: Well. That's a mighty deep subject.

GEORGE: My mother used to say that.

DR. BISCOTTI: Yes, I remember.

(He rises.)

Good luck to you, George.

GEORGE: Ah, Doc. You don't believe in luck.

DR. BISCOTTI: No. No, I don't.

GEORGE: Well... Bye.

(GEORGE exits as lights go down on his platform.)

DR. BISCOTTI: *(To audience.)* I dip biscotti into my coffee because it makes the hard cookie soft. Soft, so I can eat it more easily. I do it to make things... easier.

(He bites his biscotti.)

ABBEY: It just goes by either way, doesn't it? Time. Either way, it just goes by.

(Lights fade out.)

End of Scene 1

ACT ONE

Scene 2

SETTING: *We are still in Dr. Biscotti's office. It is one week later, Thursday at 9 am.*

AT RISE: *Lights rise on ABBEY, who is sitting in her chair on her platform with her legs tucked up to her chest. She is holding a Bible and is unable to speak. DOC is sitting in his chair and is completely focused and attentive to ABBEY. She continues to suffer in silence. DOC does nothing physically, but one gets the impression he is loving her by being as neutral a force as humanly possible. ABBEY continues to sit, perhaps with a slight rocking motion to distract the inward pain. DOC sits attentively. ABBEY rocks.*

ABBEY: *(Finally, barely getting the words out.)*
    I can't speak.
DR. BISCOTTI: All right.
ABBEY: I can't speak.
DR. BISCOTTI: Okay.
ABBEY: I can't.
DR. BISCOTTI: I'm fine.

ABBEY: *(She turns and addresses DR. BISCOTTI*
directly for the first time.)
You are?

DR. BISCOTTI: Yes.

ABBEY: Are you sure?

DR. BISCOTTI: Yes.

ABBEY: Okay.
(Silence.)
So I can just sit here and not say anything?

DR. BISCOTTI: Yes.

ABBEY: Really?
(Beat)

DR. BISCOTTI: Yes.

ABBEY: Okay.
(Beat.)
It's sort of a relief.

DR. BISCOTTI: Good.

ABBEY: 'Cause I really don't want to speak.

DR. BISCOTTI: Okay.

ABBEY: So I don't have to?

DR. BISCOTTI: No. You don't have to do anything you
don't want to do.

ABBEY: Really?

DR. BISCOTTI: Really.
(ABBEY breathes a huge but quiet sigh of relief,
and there is more silence. DR. BISCOTTI sits
attentively.)

ABBEY: It's sort of strange, don't you think, being with
somebody and not talking?

DR. BISCOTTI: How so?

ABBEY: Well, I'm here, and you're there, and no one's talking.

DR. BISCOTTI: Why is that strange?

ABBEY: Strange maybe isn't the word.

(Beat.)

Uncommon. It doesn't happen much.

DR. BISCOTTI: Why do you think that is?

ABBEY: *(She shrugs.)* Why be with someone if you're not going to talk to each other?

DR. BISCOTTI: *(He shrugs.)* Can you think of any reason?

ABBEY: No. People either talk or they do something together, but we're sitting here, and we're not doing either.

DR. BISCOTTI: We're not talking?

ABBEY: Yes, now, but not earlier. Earlier, we weren't talking at all.

DR. BISCOTTI: Hmm.

ABBEY: *(Realizing.)* And I liked that. I liked not talking.

DR. BISCOTTI: What about it did you like?

ABBEY: I'm not sure. Can we do it again?

DR. BISCOTTI: All right.

(They sit together in silence again. After about three more minutes, ABBEY becomes overwhelmed and begins to cry. DOC remains a strong, attentive force but physically does nothing.)

ABBEY: This is very odd.

DR. BISCOTTI: Odd, how so?

ABBEY: I've never done this with anyone before.

DR. BISCOTTI: So it's odd because it's new?

ABBEY: Well, not entirely. I've done it with my dog, but never with a human being.
　　　(DR. BISCOTTI nods. Silence, then suddenly...)
　　　Rose died.
　　　(ABBEY begins to cry.)
DR. BISCOTTI: I'm very sorry.
ABBEY: She died.
DR. BISCOTTI: Yes.
ABBEY: She's dead.
　　　(Beat.)
　　　Last Thursday night, after our session, after visiting the vet. I told you. Remember?
DR. BISCOTTI: Yes.
ABBEY: I went to the vet and told them what was going on with her—that she wasn't eating much, and they felt the lumps and wanted to do an x-ray. I asked how much that would cost, and they said, "Two hundred and 50 dollars." And I asked them what that would do for her, and they said that the X-ray would tell us if it was cancer or not. Two hundred and 50 dollars. Then I said, "What if it is cancer? I mean, she's 15 years old. If the X-ray shows that the lungs are filled with lumps, she's going to die, right?" And they said yes. And I said, "What happens if we don't do the x-ray? She's still going to die, right? I mean, she's 15." And they said yes. So I said, "Let's not do the x-ray." I mean, it can't all come down to money, right? I mean, that doesn't make sense. But I try to think simple, you know? I try to think simple.
DR. BISCOTTI: Yes.

ABBEY: 'Cause it's a complicated world, and things just
        keep getting more and more complicated.
DR. BISCOTTI: Yes.
ABBEY: So I said, "What should I do?" And they said,
        "Well, if you're not going to let us do the x-ray..."
        and they're trying to make me feel all badly about
        that...
DR. BISCOTTI: Good.
ABBEY: "Good" what?
DR. BISCOTTI: Good that you noticed that they were
        trying to make you feel badly about that.
ABBEY: Oh, okay.
        (Beat.)
        Why is that good?
DR. BISCOTTI: Well, it sounds like you were aware that
        you were being manipulated.
ABBEY: I was?
DR. BISCOTTI: Isn't that what you said?
ABBEY: *(Pleased.)* Yes. I think I did notice that.
        (Beat.)
        So where was I?
DR. BISCOTTI: You were telling me that you had
        decided not to let them manipulate you into
        purchasing a 250 dollar x-ray when you truthfully
        didn't need it, and you were going to tell me what
        they were going to recommend next.
ABBEY: Yes, that's right. Then they said that they could
        give her a shot of prednisone to stimulate her
        appetite and get her to eat, 'cause if she doesn't
        eat, well, she could die from that too. So I asked

them how much that would cost, and they said
15 dollars. And I said okay. Let's give her that.
(Beat.)
Money.
(She shakes her head as the tears come again.)
I mean, I'm broke. I'm on unemployment. I can't
go out of the house. But it can't come down to
money, right?
*(DR. BISCOTTI listens with compassion but says
nothing.)*

ABBEY: *(Continued.)* So they give her the shot, and we
go home. I have to sort of lift her into the car
because she's not like she used to be. She used to
jump in on her own, but not anymore. I put her
two front paws up, and then I lift up her hind
quarters and sort of...push her in 'cause she's
heavy, and I can't lift her. And she turns around
and looks at me and she knows. She looks at me
and says, "Hey, I appreciate what you're doing. I
really do." So I take her home and have
somewhat of a normal day. My unemployment
check came. I deposited it and paid my bills—
most of them. That night, I'm at my desk, and she
comes in, Rose, and she says she's gotta go out.

DR. BISCOTTI: "Says?"

ABBEY: Well, you know how animals kind of talk to you,
and you sort of know what they're saying.

DR. BISCOTTI: *(He shakes his head a bit.)*
Hmm...how does that work?

ABBEY: Well, with Rose, it's easy.

DR. BISCOTTI: How so?

ABBEY: I've not talked with you about this before?

DR. BISCOTTI: I didn't know about these conversations.

ABBEY: Well, I wouldn't really call them conversations. I just sort of know what she's thinking. What she needs. Everyone can do that with their own dog, right?

DR. BISCOTTI: I think most people only wish they could communicate with their pets.

ABBEY: I suppose that means something about me. I suppose that means I'm really screwed up.

DR. BISCOTTI: Hmm. Sounds like it could be a gift to me.

ABBEY: A gift?

(Pleased with this concept.)

Oh. Well, I can sort of do that with people, too. That's why I don't like them.

DR. BISCOTTI: All people or some people?

ABBEY: Most people. Most people. Sorry.

DR. BISCOTTI: It's okay.

ABBEY: Most people have some sort of a thing going on; they want something, and you can kind of feel it out there, and it's annoying.

DR. BISCOTTI: So that's why you don't like to go out?

ABBEY: Well, no. I thought I had that disorder. That agoraphobia.

DR. BISCOTTI: Really?

ABBEY: Didn't you tell me that?

DR. BISCOTTI: No, I never told you that. I never said anything about it.

ABBEY: Oh, well, somebody told me that.

DR. BISCOTTI: Hmm.

ABBEY: So what do you think's wrong with me?
>   *(Beat.)*
DR. BISCOTTI: Nothing.
>   *(As a matter of fact, without emotion.)*
>   Not a thing.
>   *(Lights come up on STEVE'S platform as he enters from offstage.)*
STEVE: So, nothing happened. He didn't show. Do you believe it? All that trouble and the prick never shows. Not even to watch his own mother be put into the ground. F-ing loser. Makes me think I just wasted my time.
ABBEY: Am I wasting my time, then?
DR. BISCOTTI: *(To ABBEY.)* What do you think?
STEVE: We were all braced—my brother, sisters—to expect anything, but after about half an hour into the service... Well, we all just breathed a sigh of relief and let it go. Let him go.
>   *(He sits.)*
ABBEY: *(Painfully.)* It's hard to... I'm having a hard time letting her go.
DR. BISCOTTI: *(He rises and crosses downstage to the audience.)*
>   In my practice, I have found that people basically fall into one of three categories—there are narcissists, there are those upon whom narcissists feed, and there are those who are healthy enough not to be fed upon.
>   *(Beat.)*
>   Once the people upon whom narcissists feed understand and have insight into that concept,

they want very badly to fix themselves so as to
never again fall into the devouring hands of the
energy-sucking narcissists who have been acting
like parasites on them, in most cases throughout
their entire lives.

(He crosses back to his chair, sits, and addresses
ABBEY.)

Tell me more about people.

ABBEY: I always sense they're wanting something.

DR. BISCOTTI: Always?

ABBEY: Well, when we first meet, it's okay, but shortly
afterward, there is some sort of wanting going on,
and there's a pull from them. A pull, pulling on
me.

DR. BISCOTTI: Have you figured out what that is?

ABBEY: No. No, I haven't.

DR. BISCOTTI: Okay.

ABBEY: It's just a feeling I get. I never really thought
much about it.

DR. BISCOTTI: Okay.

ABBEY: You don't think I'm making that up?

DR. BISCOTTI: Are you?

ABBEY: No.

(Considering the idea.)

So maybe people really do want something from
me?

DR. BISCOTTI: What is it you think they want?

ABBEY: I don't have anything. If I don't have anything,
what could they want?

DR. BISCOTTI: Good question.

ABBEY: So what you're saying is that there's this pull going on, and it's really happening? It's not my imagination?

(DR. BISCOTTI says nothing.)

So what's the pull?

DR. BISCOTTI: That might depend on who it is you're with. You said most people.

ABBEY: Yes. I usually come home feeling like I've got to get rid of something I've picked up. Like a disease.

DR. BISCOTTI: A disease?

ABBEY: Yes. Wash it off. I was thinking maybe I had that compulsive disorder. Didn't you tell me that once? That compulsive disorder?

DR. BISCOTTI: Did I?

ABBEY: I thought you did.

DR. BISCOTTI: Tell me more about that.

SHERIE: *(Lights up on SHERIE'S playing area as she enters from offstage.)*

Well, I'm scheduled for surgery, Monday morning. A lumpectomy. "Welcome, 40!"

(She strikes a dramatic pose.)

ABBEY: It happens a lot on dates.

SHERIE: Good thing I'm married, 'cause I'd never find anyone, now. Not with the mega-licious scar I'm going to have.

ABBEY: Dates with a man.

SHERIE: No man would want me.

ABBEY: After dates, I take a lot of baths.

SHERIE: I asked if they could make the scar so that it won't be seen beneath a bikini, and my husband said, "You're married now; you don't need to wear bikinis." I can't tell if he's trying to make me feel better or if he's becoming some sort of control nut. He's never been like this before, talking to me like that. Suddenly, he's saying strange things like, "Lose the bikini." But regardless, the scar is going to be under the breast, in the crease, and it will extend as long as a bikini top would extend, supposedly. If all goes right.

(She sits.)

ABBEY: They never go right; that's all I can say.

DR. BISCOTTI: *(To ABBEY.)* What do you mean by "right"?

ABBEY: Well, I imagine a "right" date would consist of both people talking equally. One talks, the other talks, then one talks, and the other talks, and over a period of about a two to three-hour dinner, both people sort of have an idea of who the other is.

DR. BISCOTTI: And what's "wrong"?

ABBEY: He talks, I listen. He talks, I listen. I get bored, so I force in a quick antidote or two about myself and then listen again for the rest of the date. And all the while he's talking, his mind is off thinking about something else...

STEVE: *(He rises.)* So, I'm heading out of the church, and I see this woman—attractive, wearing this flouncy thing, short. The dress, not her. And she's hanging out with my sister, so I go over to Janie

and say, "What's up?" thinking she'd introduce
me.

ABBEY: *(She rises and crosses downstage.)*
They're always thinking about something else...
I'm not sure what.

SHERIE: I'm not sure what's going on with him. He's
been acting strange ever since this whole damn
thing started. I need him to be solid now, not
some sort of control nut.

STEVE: But does she? No. Like I can control what my
sister does.
(He sits.)

DR. BISCOTTI: So, what do you think a man might want
from you on a date?

ABBEY: It's too obvious.

DR. BISCOTTI: Too obvious?

ABBEY: Yes.
(She sits.)

DR. BISCOTTI: Maybe "obvious" is right.

ABBEY: Sex.

DR. BISCOTTI: Sex. Okay.

ABBEY: So I'm not making that up?

DR. BISCOTTI: Uh, no. I think you're probably right on
the money with this one. Do you give them what
they want?

STEVE: Does she give me what I want?

ABBEY: Yes.

STEVE: No.

DR. BISCOTTI: *(To ABBEY.)* Why?

ABBEY: I don't know.

STEVE: I don't know why I bother.

28

ABBEY: I don't know why.

STEVE: *(He rises.)* I've never been able to make anything work with a woman for more than two or three months at a time, but there's something about this woman...

(He uses his right arm to emphasize what it is he's saying, which happens to be in the direction of where SHERIE is sitting on stage.)

...a connection I feel, and I can't get her off my mind the entire afternoon. We drive over to the graveside, and my siblings and my mom are standing there beside me, but my mind is... Well, I'm looking over at this woman in this black and white, very short, polka-dotted dress. She's got on these heels, black heels, and she's sinking into the dirt, getting shorter and shorter by the minute, and the more she shrinks, the more confident I get, 'cause hell, I'm taller than her now. I decide to hit her up at my mom's house 'cause if she's at the graveside, willing to sink in the mud, she'll be at my mom's.

(He sits.)

SHERIE: *(She rises.)* I took off from work yesterday—the whole day. I didn't feel like going in. Thought I'd... I don't know, go buy a hat or something, but instead, I end up down in our basement looking through old photo albums, from high school mostly. I open the books, and notice this yellow thing going on, you know? The pages. They were yellowing, and the photos had begun to fade away. Some of them were nearly all faded. Who

the hell knows where the negatives are. I don't.
So I take them down to...that store. You know
—the pharmacy that still develops photographs.
Anyway, I say look at this. What's going on here?
And they say, "Acid. These are not acid-free
pages." Well, who in the world knew about acid-
free pages back then?! I didn't know about acid-
free pages! And now all my memories are fading
because I didn't know about acid-free pages!
Fading! They're all just fading away!!

ABBEY: If I knew why, why I did it, maybe I wouldn't do
it anymore.

SHERIE: But I still have good legs.

ABBEY: Maybe I wouldn't.

SHERIE: *(She sits.)* I'm wearing the turtlenecks to get
my friends and family used to seeing me in them
prior to my neck and chest turning into the
nightmare God intended to torture me with. But,
my legs are still very good.

ABBEY: *(She rises and faces downstage left.)*
I was standing in the grocery store, buying soy
milk, and there was this man behind me.
(She sets this up for us, physically.)
I didn't know he was there for sure, but I felt him.
Before I turned and looked, I felt him there,
staring at me.

SHERIE: I had to go to this...
(It's difficult for her to say.)
...event. This...you know, event, which is partly
why I didn't go into work. And the only thing I
had in black was one of my cocktail dresses from

my pre-marital days. Charles doesn't like when I wear my dresses too short.

ABBEY: The line was long.

SHERIE: Short, you know. He doesn't like it.

ABBEY: *(Reiterating.)* Long.

SHERIE: I don't know if that's fair to say. He doesn't think I need to wear short dresses because he says it makes a statement about me that I shouldn't be making now that I'm married. Something like that.

ABBEY: So, I'm standing in the line minding my own business, and I feel this sensation...below.

DR. BISCOTTI: Sensation?

SHERIE: I like wearing short dresses because of the feeling I get when my legs rub up against each other. I feel sexy. I feel like I have something of value to offer.

ABBEY: Yes, sensation. Below. In my...area.

DR. BISCOTTI: Area?

ABBEY: Yes, you know.

DR. BISCOTTI: Area?

ABBEY: My...area.

DR. BISCOTTI: *(Understanding.)* Oh, okay.

ABBEY: Yeah.

SHERIE: Can I talk with you about this?

ABBEY: Can I talk with you about this?

DR. BISCOTTI: *(To ABBEY.)* Yes.

ABBEY: I'm standing there looking forward, holding the lettuce and the soy milk, and I'm feeling aroused. I'm getting aroused.

DR. BISCOTTI: Yes.

ABBEY: *(With a bit of a twinkle in her eye.)*
  And it wasn't the lettuce.
DR. BISCOTTI: *(Smiling.)* Not the lettuce.
ABBEY: No. I'm feeling aroused, and I turn slightly to
  my right, and there's this guy looking at me from
  behind, and I mean, he's looking at me, and I
  realize it's coming from him, you see?
DR. BISCOTTI: The arousal?
ABBEY: Yes, exactly! He had his own thing going on.
DR. BISCOTTI: His own thing.
ABBEY: Yes.
DR. BISCOTTI: Not yours.
ABBEY: No, *his*.
STEVE: If she didn't have on that dress I might not have
  bothered at all.
ABBEY: Yes, and I'm picking up on it, you see? I
  automatically start thinking it's *my* feeling, that it
  started with me when it really didn't. It started
  with him. *It's his.*
  (She sits.)
  It's not that I'm trying to place the blame
  somewhere else. It's just I'm thinking now, if this
  is real, if I'm not imagining it, then maybe I'm
  picking up on other things too. Not just that my
  dog is about to die... And the problem is, I don't
  just pick up on these things—I literally pick
  them up!
DR. BISCOTTI: Like a disease.
ABBEY: Exactly! And then I have to go home and wash it
  off.

SHERIE: *(She notices that there is mud around the bottom of her high-heeled shoes.)*
Oh, look at this. I forgot to wash these off. Dear, Lord.
(She takes a Kleenex out of her purse and wets it with her saliva. She then proceeds to wipe the dirt off from around her heels.)
You want to know something I find very odd? If you look at a graveyard, which God knows I want nothing to do with them, but objectively speaking—look at a graveyard. The people who tend to them, the gardeners? They water like crazy around the grave sites that are new—that are about to be visited by the current "suffering family." They water till the grass is floating in the dirt. It looks good, but it's floating.

STEVE: So I don't know who she is. All I know is that she is gorgeous.

SHERIE: *(Rises.)* So I'm standing there in this floating sod, this over-watered grass...sinking.

STEVE: *(He rises.)* Suddenly, she takes off her shoes. and I thought I'd lose my f-ing mind.

SHERIE: They're Italian. I'm not going to stand there and ruin a perfectly good pair of Italian shoes.

STEVE: She takes them off!

SHERIE: So I take them off.

DR. BISCOTTI: *(He rises and crosses to STEVE and SHERIE, to them.)*
Wait. Wait. Whose funeral was this?
(STEVE and SHERIE do not hear DR. BISCOTTI.)

STEVE: I decide not to wait to see if she shows up at Mom's place. Don't want to chance it. We all read something from the Bible, then ashes to ashes, and I head on over.

(He steps downstage right on his platform, closer to SHERIE, not knowing she's there.)

DR. BISCOTTI: Dear God.

(He turns away from them.)

ABBEY: *(To DR. BISCOTTI.)* Are you all right?

SHERIE: And this guy I've never met before in my life walks up to me and tells me that he's lost something in the grass and could I help him find it.

DR. BISCOTTI: *(To self.)* Oh, no.

(He crosses away, to his desk.)

ABBEY: Dr. Biscotti?

SHERIE: I start helping him look for it; I bend over to look in the grass below and ask him, "So, what did you lose?" And he says, "My smile."

STEVE: Her smile.

ABBEY: *(To DR. BISCOTTI.)* Maybe you'd feel better if you ate something.

SHERIE: And, of course, this makes me smile.

ABBEY: How 'bout your cookie there? Dr. Biscotti?

DR. BISCOTTI: *(He crosses downstage, then to the audience.)*

We as humans seem to thrive when we receive any hope whatsoever that a pattern of synchronicity exists in the midst of our day-to-day mundane chaos. Coincidence seems necessary because of our human condition.

(Beat.)

We need to know that there is something larger and more knowledgeable than ourselves who is overseeing things, who has our best interest at heart, and to whatever degree, this "entity" is orchestrating things so that our lives are improved. This can be very dangerous because a coincidence doesn't always mean there's order or that a change in that direction would be for the overall good.

(SHERIE, STEVE, and ABBEY methodically return to their seats on each of their own platforms. DR. BISCOTTI crosses and sits on the downstage lip of the desk.)

There's a story of a fellow in the late 1800s, a man by the name of Henry Ziegland. He broke up with his girlfriend, and because of this, she committed suicide. Well, this didn't make the girl's brother very happy. He bought a gun and shot Ziegland and then shot and killed himself. But when the dust cleared, Ziegland was not dead. The bullet had grazed his head and lodged itself into a very large tree. Ziegland breathed a sigh of relief and went about his life. Years later, he decided that he would cut down that very large tree, which still had the bullet lodged in it. Because the tree was so very large, he chose to use dynamite, and the explosion propelled the bullet out of the tree and into Ziegland's head and killed him.

(Lights slowly fade out as we hear Roy Orbison singing a rendition of his provocative song "Dream Baby" or a similar song.)

End of Act One

ACT TWO

Scene 1

SETTING: DR. BISCOTTI'S office, Thursday at 9
            am, one week later.

AT RISE: Lights come up on DOC, who is sitting
            behind his desk, and SHERIE, who is
            now sitting on the platform just to DR.
            BISCOTTI'S left—ABBEY'S old platform.
            There is no one else on stage.

SHERIE: *(SHERIE talks to DR. BISCOTTI, but with
        very little eye contact.)*
        He's about 30...maybe. Six feet tall, dirty blonde
        hair or brown maybe, solid—the strong type, you
        know. We just met for coffee. No big deal.
        Nothing wrong with just meeting for coffee. He
        buys, which I love, and...we talk.
DR. BISCOTTI: *(Knowing she won't hear him.)*
        You took off your wedding ring, didn't you?
SHERIE: *(She does not hear him and continues to talk.)*
        He told me about his grandmother and how she
        lived this great life and got to die in the house
        she grew up in.
DR. BISCOTTI: *(To self.)* She took off her wedding ring.
SHERIE: He talked about his diet—no soda, no dairy,
        and his workout routine—not missing a day, ever,

not once…and taking whey. Whey protein powder, I think he said.

(*Beat.*)

I didn't tell him about my surgery because, heck, I mean, it went fine, and you can't notice.

(*She rises and pulls the turtleneck snugly against her chest.*)

The bandages are still…there, but I was able to put a bra over it all, and you can't tell. The bandages have to stay on for a week, so…just a couple more days, and then we take them off and…get to have a "look-see."

(*With fragility.*)

I'm thinking that if my bra fits me with the bandages on, that well… I'm figuring they took out quite a bit, you know? I'm thinking they removed quite a bit.

DR. BISCOTTI: That might be.

SHERIE: (*She doesn't hear him.*) I don't know.

(*Lost in thought.*)

I just never really thought this would happen. To me. I don't know why I thought that. It makes no sense to think that 'cause I've gone through this with my mother and my friend, Jackie, but I just never thought…

(*She stops, then brushes it off and continues.*)

So, we're sitting there, and he, uh, notices that I…

DR. BISCOTTI: …have a wedding band on.

SHERIE: (*Not hearing him.*) That I have shaved my legs.

DR. BISCOTTI: That you've shaved your legs.

SHERIE: And he leans in and says, "Did you do that for me?"

DR. BISCOTTI: Oh, dear.

SHERIE: And I just smiled, you know. And he says, "I've got to tell you—you have the most gorgeous smile." And he puts his hand on my knee, just my knee, and uh, well... I haven't gotten that excited since...well, high school. And I'm sorry, but this feels so good. I'm sorry. You know? It feels so damn good.

DR. BISCOTTI: I see.

SHERIE: My husband gives me nothing. Says nothing. He's sort of removed himself from the situation. He comes home from work now and just sits there...reading Golf magazine and...what am I supposed to do? I talk with him, *to* him, and he says nothing.

DR. BISCOTTI: Why do you think that is?

SHERIE: *(She doesn't listen.)* I don't get it.

DR. BISCOTTI: Maybe he's learned.

SHERIE: I sit there for a while trying to converse, waiting for him to notice that I am having a hard time and want to talk, but he just reads. I go to bed and cry myself to sleep. All the while wishing he would crawl up behind me and hold me and tell me he loves me just the way I am, but he just sits there reading all night long. I want to call out to him and tell him how I'm hurting but...I can't. I can't open my mouth and ask...

DR. BISCOTTI: Why not? Why not?

SHERIE: *(She continues, not hearing him.)*

So, I call up this fellow. He'd given me his number at the...event.

(Recognizing that she's being ridiculous. It's just a word.)

Funeral. At the funeral. And I called him up and say, "Let's meet, have some java, a few laughs." And it was...very refreshing. Really. Very...

(SHERIE suddenly stops talking, rises, and pulls her sweater tight against her figure. She then turns to DR. BISCOTTI for the first time and addresses him directly.)

Do you notice a difference?

(She continues to pull the sweater so it is snug against her skin.)

Doc?

DR. BISCOTTI: *(A bit surprised.)* Pardon?

SHERIE: *(With vulnerability.)* Do I look differently to you?

DR. BISCOTTI: Your physical persona or you as a person?

SHERIE: *(With growing anger.)* Oh, well. "My physical persona!" My body! Specifically my fucking breast. Does my fucking breast look different to you?

(DOC remains unmoved with a slightly saddened expression on his face. She watches him. He says nothing.)

I'm very sorry. Very sorry.

(She doesn't know what to say.)

I've hired you to help me. I pay you very good money, and then I go and yell at you like that. I'm really very sorry.

(She sits and continues with difficulty.)

You know, I didn't expect them to take away half my breast. I didn't. I mean, the lump is big. Was. Big, but I didn't think they'd take a bunch of other stuff with it, you know? I uh...don't know what I was thinking, but I wasn't thinking half.

(She chuckles.)

So, turtle necks are out. You know what I'm saying, Doc? They're out. Unless I get some sort of a special bra-type thing, but when that's taken off in the heat of passion... Well, who knows what you'll see.

(Beat.)

The Wicked Witch of the West.

(Beat.)

Anyway, I didn't go home with him if that's what you're thinking.

(Caring about what he thinks, she watches him.)

Is it? Is that what you were thinking I'd do?

(A beat.)

DR. BISCOTTI: No.

SHERIE: *(With vulnerability.)* Really?

DR. BISCOTTI: No. I didn't think you would, Sherie.

SHERIE: *(SHERIE sits and starts to cry.)*

It was awful. The surgery. Just awful. I think they gave me too much anesthetic, and I wouldn't wake up. I could not wake up. When I did, they filled me with hot tea and peanut butter crackers,

which I do not normally eat—peanut butter crackers —the store-bought kind in those wrappers. I guess I was the last surgery of the day, and the nurse wanted to go home, you know? She just wanted to go home, and I wasn't peeing, so she had to make me pee. Once I peed, she could go home and be with her kids and husband and live some sort of...normal life.
(An aside.)
Bitch.
(She rises out of the chair as if it is the hospital bed.)
I get out of the hospital bed to walk to the bathroom; finally, my husband is holding me to help steady me, and I take three steps...
(She takes three steps downstage.)
...and I puke all over his feet. All over his feet. And he didn't move. He didn't move a muscle. He stayed beside me, holding me, with puke all over his feet.
(Crying.)
And then I go and meet this...jerk, really, this self-absorbed jerk for coffee, and I actually think about screwing him.
(Full of pain.)
I mean, what's up with that?
(She crosses to DOC and really asks the question.)
What is up with that?!
(DR. BISCOTTI takes a breath.)

42

DR. BISCOTTI: "I do not understand what I do. For what I want to do, I do not do, but what I hate, I do."

SHERIE: Pardon?

DR. BISCOTTI: *(He offers her one of his cookies.)* Biscotti?

SHERIE: Oh.

(She sits.)

DR. BISCOTTI: It beats store-packaged peanut butter crackers.

SHERIE: *(She smiles.)* Sure.

(She takes a cookie, bites into it, then reacts to its hardness.)

DR. BISCOTTI: Coffee?

SHERIE: Yeah. Thanks.

(DOC pours her a cup of java. She dips the biscotti into the coffee and bites again.)

Ah, very good.

DR. BISCOTTI: Yes.

SHERIE: Why is that so amazingly good?

DR. BISCOTTI: I'm not sure.

(A bit of silence while they eat and drink together.)

SHERIE: I guess this is all just about me being afraid to die, isn't it?

DR. BISCOTTI: Or...age.

SHERIE: Ahhh, yes—that. Aging.

DR. BISCOTTI: How 'bout we start with that, and then next week we'll work on you being okay with dying?

SHERIE: *(She laughs.)* Okay.

(SHERIE and DOC sit together dipping and sipping when ABBEY enters and crosses to the platform just to DR. BISCOTTI'S right, where STEVE used to be.)

ABBEY: *(Lights up. She talks to DR. BISCOTTI as if he's out over the audience.)*

You're never going to believe what I did. Never. Not in a million years.

(She breathes.)

Today, I parked in a brand new spot. Most every time I've come here, for the past however many years, I've parked in the same spot, on the opposite side of the street. Don't know why, I just have. I used to have to cross the street to get into the building, so it didn't make any sense. But today, I pull up to the building, and it occurred to me that there is plenty of room right here, on this side of the street, so just for the heck of it, I thought I'd try something different. It did occur to me, while I was doing it, that I was trying something different, something new, and I did it anyway. In fact, I did it because it was new, kind of thinking in the back of my mind that maybe something different would happen if I did, you know? Like maybe during the day, today, some more different things would happen, and I was excited about that. That thought never occurred to me before, that I could choose a different spot. Cool, huh?

DR. BISCOTTI: *(To SHERIE.)* Would you like another?

SHERIE: No, thank you.

ABBEY: And you know what's even cooler than that? That "thought" did not come from anyone but me. Me! I made sure of it. That thought came right from me!

(She sits.)

SHERIE: So, where were we?

DR. BISCOTTI: *(To SHERIE.)* Starbucks. You were telling me about Steve?

SHERIE: Steve? Did I mention his name?

(Silence.)

DR. BISCOTTI: I thought you did.

SHERIE: Well, I guess I must have.

ABBEY: I'm very happy about this.

SHERIE: He wasn't very happy. But I'll only take responsibility for some of that...rage. I don't know where he got the rest.

DR. BISCOTTI: It's hard to say.

SHERIE: *(She sets her cup of coffee down at the foot of her chair.)*

I thanked him for the coffee but told him that I felt we should not see each other again.

DR. BISCOTTI: I see.

ABBEY: Very happy.

SHERIE: And he very abruptly pushed the table away from him and said, "Well, fuck you." Just like that, "Fuck you." Very strange. Why would someone do that?

DR. BISCOTTI: Why do you think?

SHERIE: If I hadn't finished my coffee, it would have spilled all over my new skirt. And then he would have seen some rage, that's what I think!

(She shrugs.)

And then he stormed out.

ABBEY: I've been watching people, you know? Watching them and seeing what they do, not what they say, not all the flattery things they say to make you feel good, but what they do. I saw this thing on 60 Minutes where most of our communication is non-verbal, like 95 percent, so I thought I'd learn more if I watched.

SHERIE: *(Gathers her purse.)* He sure wasn't what I thought he was.

ABBEY: People aren't what they say they are.

SHERIE: *(Writes out a check.)* A narrow escape.

DR. BISCOTTI: Sounds like it.

SHERIE: I don't know what I was thinking.

ABBEY: Life has taken an interesting turn.

SHERIE: *(Hands check to DR. BISCOTTI.)* So, I'll see you next week?

DR. BISCOTTI: I appreciate you being flexible with your appointment time.

SHERIE: No problem. I'm just going into work late instead of taking off early for lunch. Worked out fine.

DR. BISCOTTI: *(He rises and takes the check.)* So, next week at nine, then.

SHERIE: See you then.

(SHERIE exits. DR. BISCOTTI places the check into his appointment book.)

ABBEY: *(ABBEY turns and talks directly to DR. BISCOTTI.)* I caught it whispering in my ear.

DR. BISCOTTI: *(He crosses to the front of his desk and sits, then to ABBEY...)*
Whispering? Who?

ABBEY: The dark force. I actually caught it red-handed. This morning. I got to sleep in a little longer because I didn't have to leave my house till nine-thirty, and I'm lying in bed not quite awake, and I felt something near my left ear—a voice, a breath of air, a little puff of energy and I heard it say, "You are worthless. You have no worth whatsoever." But I heard it before it became my thought. Before I adopted it as my own. I caught it, you see?

DR. BISCOTTI: Tell me more.

ABBEY: I caught it whispering in my ear and realized it's not me. It's something outside of me. And it lies.

DR. BISCOTTI: It lies?

ABBEY: Yes, exactly. It lies, and I used to believe it, but not anymore.

DR. BISCOTTI: *(Not hearing her the first time.)* What did it say to you?

ABBEY: It said that I was worthless, that I had no value, and I know that's not true.

DR. BISCOTTI: Well, this is amazing, don't you think?

ABBEY: Really? That's what I was thinking. I could barely wait to get in here this morning, to tell you, but I thought you might think I was a bit off-center.
(She rises.)
I must have some value, some reason for being here, or I wouldn't be here, right? So it's a lie.

DR. BISCOTTI: Yes, I believe there's a reason for you
being here.

ABBEY: *(Quickly.)* I love to paint. Did you know that?

DR. BISCOTTI: No. You have not shared that with me.

ABBEY: Well, it's true. I love to paint, and the reason I
love to paint is because when I do it, I don't hear
any whispering going on—nothing. I hear
silences, one after the other.

(Beat.)

But not before I start.

(She sits back in her chair.)

Before I start, I hear things like, "Why waste your
time? You'll never sell this? No one would ever
pay you money for this piece of crap," even
though I hadn't even painted anything yet, the
voice would tell me it's no good. And the next
thing you know, I stopped painting. Haven't
painted in years. But now I know where it's
coming from, and it ain't me.

(Defiantly.)

I like to paint, and there's no good reason why I
shouldn't.

DR. BISCOTTI: I agree.

ABBEY: So I dug into my closet and pulled out my old
paints—acrylic, so they're still good, and my
brushes and my pallet and threw something up,
nothing amazing, but I heard the voices, and I did
it anyway. I heard them, knew where they were
coming from, and I did it anyway.

*(She rises and crosses to look out the imaginary
window.)*

The painting's in the car. I brought it with me 'cause I was thinking that I would take it down to the farmer's market and see if I could sell it. I might. You never know.

DR. BISCOTTI: You never know.

ABBEY: Stranger things have happened.

DR. BISCOTTI: They have. That's not so strange.

ABBEY: Nope.

> *(Beat.)*
> They're open on Thursdays, right?
> *(STEVE enters from offstage and steps onto SHERIE'S old platform, far stage right.)*

DR. BISCOTTI: I think so.

ABBEY: *(ABBEY, on the platform between STEVE and DR. BISCOTTI, does not see STEVE but senses his presence.)*
> I told you about that guy at Whole Foods, right? That guy standing behind me in line?

DR. BISCOTTI: Yes. Last week.

ABBEY: Hmm.

DR. BISCOTTI: What?

ABBEY: I just remembered what he was buying.

DR. BISCOTTI: What?

ABBEY: I've always been curious about that—how things pop into your head out of nowhere.

DR. BISCOTTI: Yes. You had the lettuce.

ABBEY: *(Smiling at his comment but continuing.)*
> Yes, I had the lettuce, but he was buying some sort of protein powder, you know? For bodybuilders. And I thought, "What a stupid jock." Isn't that weird that that would pop into

my head just now? "Whey." It said "whey" on the bottle.

STEVE: *(Lights come up on STEVE'S platform. He addresses DR. BISCOTTI as if he is out over the audience. Something is different about him. Something has changed.)*
Well, I'm here. I can see you still refuse to roll out the red carpet.

ABBEY: But that was the beginning, really, of me figuring this all out, so that's good. However strange, it's good.

STEVE: I'm starting to think these talks aren't getting me anywhere.

ABBEY: I don't know where I'd be without our talks. Without you.

DR. BISCOTTI: *(Genuinely.)* Well, thank you, Abbey. *(...but with boundaries. He rises.)*
I'll see you next week then?

ABBEY: Yes, 10 o'clock. I get to sleep in. Or paint! *(She picks up her purse and turns to go.)*
I feel this weird thing when I have to go.

DR. BISCOTTI: Weird today or weird *every time* you're about to leave one of our sessions?

ABBEY: Ummm, every time, I guess. It's odd having to leave after being able to be so...myself with you. Then to have to leave and become all careful again.

DR. BISCOTTI: The world seems to require "carefulness," doesn't it?

ABBEY: Yes, it does.
(Beat.)

Take care of yourself, okay? Take care.

DR. BISCOTTI: Yes, thank you. You too.

> *(She exits hesitantly. DOC sips his cold coffee. He reacts to its unpleasant temperature. And his biscotti is gone. The next seven lines overlap.)*

STEVE: I needed to cancel my appointment today because I know you have that 24-hour thing about canceling, but I called you, and your answering service wasn't working.

DR. BISCOTTI: That's strange.

STEVE: *(Not hearing him.)* I tried. A couple of times.

DR. BISCOTTI: It's been working for everyone else who has called today.

STEVE: *(Not hearing him.)* I don't know what's up with that, but what can I say?

DR. BISCOTTI: I've received 10 or 12 messages today, at least.

STEVE: *(Continuing and not hearing.)* I didn't want to just not show up. I know how that can be, but I really can't meet today if that's okay.

DR. BISCOTTI: I'm sure something very important's come up for you, so of course it's okay...

STEVE: Great!

DR. BISCOTTI: ...but because you didn't give me the 24-hour notice, you're still going to have to pay me for the full session.

STEVE: Shit!

> *(Pause.)*

DR. BISCOTTI: Sorry. You know the rules.

STEVE: *(Suddenly angry, he kicks the chair, and it falls over.)*

Fuck the rules!

DR. BISCOTTI: Rules are sometimes hard to follow, and
I want to remind you...

STEVE: *(He hits the wall.)* Shit!

DR. BISCOTTI: ...if you become threatening, I'm going
to have to ask you to leave.

STEVE: So, let me get this straight—I have to stay
because I have to pay, but I have to leave because
I might become threatening?

DR. BISCOTTI: Yes, that's right.

STEVE: So, I don't seem to have much choice.

DR. BISCOTTI: Well, you do, actually. You can stay, or
you can go, but there are rules and consequences
that go along with both choices.

STEVE: *(Another outburst.)* Fuck.
(Beat.)
Sorry. Sorry. I'll stay.
(Calming himself down.)
I can stay.
(He picks up the chair and sits in it.)

DR. BISCOTTI: All right.
(He sits to begin.)

STEVE: I don't throw away money, Doc. I can't. Not like
your other clients.

DR. BISCOTTI: *(Quickly.)* Do you know any of my other
clients?
(Beat.)

STEVE: No. I'm just saying.

DR. BISCOTTI: Because it's important for me to
maintain an environment of confidentiality.

STEVE: *(He rises and crosses upstage his platform.)*

I'm just saying from my view point I don't have much choice in the matter.

(Beat.)

'Cause I'm not going to throw away the money.

DR. BISCOTTI: That sounds like a viable choice.

STEVE: *(Shakes his head, then with sudden anger.)*
Choice. That's bullshit.

(He kicks the chair again.)

DR. BISCOTTI: *(He stands.)* Okay, it's time for you to go.

STEVE: *(Angrily.)* No. No, I'm not leaving.

(Suddenly tears, and desperation.)

I can't. *I can't.*

DR. BISCOTTI: *(Trying to remain calm but holding his boundary as best he can.)*
Okay. You get one more chance, Steve. One more.

STEVE: *(Fast to comply, he picks up the chair.)*
All right. All right. All right.

(He sits.)

DR. BISCOTTI: *(Seeing STEVE sit, he then sits.)*
If I don't set effective boundaries for you, our sessions will not be beneficial. It's for your care and safety. And if I don't look out for you, then I'm not doing my job. The rules are for your good...and mine.

STEVE: *(Calming down, genuine.)* Oh, I know. I know. I just get upset when I'm told that I have "choice." I don't see much choice in the world. I'm told it's there, but I just don't see it. That's all.

DR. BISCOTTI: Do you want to talk about that?

STEVE: No. No, I do not want to talk about that. Quite
honestly, I'm tired of talking about that and this,
and this and that. It's gotten me nowhere. I can't
do anything better than I could three months ago,
except now everything's worse. It's worse.
"Express yourself. Talk about your feelings." It's
all a bunch of...
(Makes the choice to not say bullshit.)
...malarkey. Everything's worse! I don't see much
of a point if everything is worse.
(He shakes his head.)
Malarkey.

DR. BISCOTTI: Sometimes, things get worse in order for
them to get better.

STEVE: And sometimes things get worse just before the
lights go out.

DR. BISCOTTI: Or you run out of milk.

STEVE: Fuuuck.
(Silence.)
Is that what you're going to do now? Torture me
'cause I'm f-ing trapped in here?
(Telling him adamantly.)
I don't want to talk bout it. If I did, I would have
walked in here like a normal little boy with his
tail tucked between his legs and behaved himself,
now wouldn't I?

DR. BISCOTTI: How does a normal little boy behave?

STEVE: Oh, God!

DR. BISCOTTI: Simple question.

STEVE: *(Painfully.)* Well, then, there must be a simple
answer, right?!

(Pause.)

DR. BISCOTTI: *(Conceding, with compassion.)*
Maybe not.

STEVE: That's right! "Maybe not!" Maybe it's not so
simple! If it were simple—life?—then I would get
what I wanted, wouldn't I? I would get what I
wanted, not right away, but with a little hard
work, over time, I would sometimes get what I
wanted, but I don't. I don't get what I want. Not
sometimes, not ever. It's not in the plan for me.
Now, some might say that's a choice. Some
would. But it isn't always a choice. Not
everything, not always. It sometimes comes down
to other things, things you can't control.
Sometimes, things you can't even see coming.
(Beat.)
Other people, for no apparent reason, walk away
with the new car and the pretty girl, but I get the
truck that breaks down, and there's nothing I can
do about it. And it always breaks down when you
need it most.
(Shakes his head.)
It always breaks down when you need it most.

DR. BISCOTTI: *(Compassionately.)* Yes.
*(STEVE looks at DR. BISCOTTI for the first
time.)*

STEVE: Dare I tell you about my day? Dare I tell you?
(DR. BISCOTTI is listening.)
You said "confidential," so what do you mean by
that? Does that mean that what you and I talk

about in here... It's just between you and me, right?

DR. BISCOTTI: *(Reassuring.)* Yes. You have the right to expect absolute privacy and confidentiality. I am prevented by law from discussing information you share with me, during our sessions, with anyone else.

STEVE: That's true?

DR. BISCOTTI: Yes. Absolutely.

STEVE: *(He begins the story.)*

My dad called yesterday. Out of the blue. Calls me up and tells me he wants to see me. Not my siblings—my brother or sisters—me. I didn't tell them because I didn't want to screw up their day too. I mean, who knows if he's going to show or not. And I'm curious. No denying that. Otherwise, I'd tell him to go to hell. I'm wondering what he looks like, if I look like him, his mannerisms. Are they the same as mine? So I agree to meet him. He lives up in this trailer park —"Sunny Acres" in Bakersfield. Not far. I was there in no time. The drive was too fast, really, didn't give me time to think or to slow down my thinking, like you've been working with me on. That might have helped, had the drive been longer.

(STEVE rises and crosses a bit downstage right on his small platform. DR. BISCOTTI rises at the same time, as STEVE is talking, and crosses downstage left of his own platform, still intently listening.)

I wasn't sure what to expect—his house. I had no idea how long he'd lived there if he remarried. No idea what to expect. I could have other brothers, sisters... I pull up into the driveway, and he's standing out front, smoking. He smelled like smoke and was all skinny, worse than I imagined. Bottles everywhere, lying around, broken.

DR. BISCOTTI: *(To audience.)* There are some people who believe that narcissists are evil. I wonder if that's true.

STEVE: He invites me in for coffee, and I'm thinking, "Okay, this ain't bad." We go in, and there's... trash everywhere. He's some kind of hoarder, you know? Junk. Magazines, old chewing tobacco cans, piled up in corners and walkways. Junk. No one in their right mind would save this crap. *(Addressing DR. BISCOTTI as if he is still sitting in his chair behind his desk.)* And I'm thinking, "This is my dad. My father." And I'm having a hard time with that. I really fucking am.

DR. BISCOTTI: *(To audience.)* Because of our human condition, we humans have a tendency to get anxious. But the presence of anxiety does not have to influence our choices, our behavior.

STEVE: *(He sits back down again.)* We sit down at this table, this table that he must have set up that morning, with pull-out legs, and he's got these two chairs he must have scrounged from some dump. You could tell he tried to sand 'em but gave up. Too hard. Too time-consuming.

(Beat.)

Too lazy. Probably never finished anything in his life. And I'm expecting him to ask me to forgive him, you know? Ask me, tell me he's sorry or something. I don't know.

DR. BISCOTTI: Yes.

STEVE: So we're sitting there and just talking about the weather, which is driving me crazy. He said he likes it when it's dry because he gets less mucus in his throat, so he sleeps better at night, and I'm sitting there, looking at his throat, you know, just staring at his throat. It's all wrinkled and old and skinny, and I'm thinking...I could just reach across this table, place my hands around his neck, and slowly squeeze the life right out of him. Just squeeze. Squeeze his throat like an overripe orange. I wouldn't even have to get up from my seat for balance or extra strength. I could just do it right from here, right now, just reach across and...

(Beat.)

Doc?

DR. BISCOTTI: Yes?

STEVE: Is it stuffy in here, or is it just me?

DR. BISCOTTI: Oh. Well, I seem to be fine.

STEVE: Okay, just checking. Do you have any water or anything?

DR. BISCOTTI: No, I'm sorry.

(Crosses back to his desk.)

There's some in the waiting room.

STEVE: No, that's okay. Just checking.

DR. BISCOTTI: *(He sits.)* So, you were saying...?

STEVE: Yeah. Yeah.

> *(He rises, nervously.)*
>
> I would like to fix things, you know? My life. I really would... I came in here, willingly, on my own because I thought it would help me with my anger, you know? I think that says a lot—me coming in here on my own.

DR. BISCOTTI: Yes.

STEVE: It was on my own, 'cause I've always had this sort of...out-of-control-thing going on, so I guess in many ways I, uh...

> *(He trails off on his own.)*

DR. BISCOTTI: Yes, it was your choice.

STEVE: *(The word "choice" is not his favorite. He reacts, then sits.)*

> So anyways, he says that he's trying to improve his life, you know? Wants to fix up the trailer, and would I help him? And I'm thinking, "Hell, no. I'm not going to help you fix up this pigsty," but that's not what he meant. What he meant is that he wanted some money. Some money! Do you believe that crap? He actually wanted me to give him 500 dollars so he could fix up his dump-of-a-trailer. Says he wants to take home some woman he met down at the local club, and there was no room for that. Says he needs more room *for that* and could I help him by giving him some

money. And I'm sitting there with my truck parked out front...

(He rises and crosses downstage to an imaginary window.)

...my truck that needs a new timing belt, and I'm thinking, "Fuck you." That's what I was thinking, "Fuck you."

(He sits.)

And I see him, sitting there all calm, and I'm thinking there's a price to pay for that calm, you mother fucker. I don't get to have that calm because you walked out on us, on me, and now I walk around with this, this bullshit inside of me, and you get to be all calm, and I said to him, "There's a price to pay for that calm," and I reach across the table, and I grabbed his throat with my two hands, and I fucking squeezed the life right out of the mother-fucking-prick.

(Silence.)

DR. BISCOTTI: Okay.

(Trying to remain calm.)

STEVE: And I am feeling...calm. For the first time in my life, I'm calm.

DR. BISCOTTI: Yes.

STEVE: So I get into my truck and head on back to the valley and while I'm driving down the grapevine, the engine falls out of my truck. Just falls right out on the freeway, and I pull over and had to tow it to the local garage, and it took them till this morning to get it fixed, so that's why I didn't... well.

(Beat.)

So it's all pretty messed up, and I can't even
believe I'm sitting here. I've never had anyone,
you see?

(Almost starts to cry.)

I've never had anyone before I could share this...
stuff with, and I guess I'm...

(Almost tears.)

Well, anyway, that's it. That's all I got to say.

(A bit tired.)

DR. BISCOTTI: All right. Well... Uh...

*(DR. BISCOTTI moves the clock on his desk just
slightly so he can see the time.)*

I guess that ends our session for today. I really
appreciate you being flexible with your schedule,
Steve. Can we meet again next week...same time?

STEVE: *(Not moving.)* Really? Are you kidding? I just
told you I killed my father.

DR. BISCOTTI: Yes. Yes, you did. And I have to tell you,
that is a lot to take in, for anyone to take in, and I
could use some time.

STEVE: *(Genuinely pleading, desperately.)*

Doc. Doc. I need your help. I don't know what to
do. I left him there at the table, slumped over at
that table, and I don't—

DR. BISCOTTI: Yes, I hear that. And I understand your
concerns, but the reality is...

(He rises.)

...I have an appointment now, coming in very
soon, and uh...this is too important—what you've
shared with me, and I don't want to address

something of this magnitude with some sort of a rushed-type environment.

STEVE: We need time.

DR. BISCOTTI: Yes, absolutely. So, if we can put this subject, regardless of how overwhelming it feels for you, if we can just put this on hold... In fact, are you free tomorrow?

(He looks at his appointment book.)

Can you come in tomorrow?

STEVE: What time?

DR. BISCOTTI: *(DR. BISCOTTI looks in his schedule book.)*

Two. Two pm?

STEVE: *(Nodding his head.)* Yes, I can be here.

DR. BISCOTTI: Great. Two pm, then.

(DR. BISCOTTI writes the time into his scheduling book.)

We will meet and pick up right where we left off.

STEVE: Okay.

(He rises.)

Until then, uh... What should I...?

DR. BISCOTTI: Go home and try to get some sleep. Eat, if you can, and just try to relax. I will see you tomorrow at two.

STEVE: *(So vulnerable, with difficulty.)* Hey, thanks, Doc. Thanks so much. I uh... I really appreciate it.

DR. BISCOTTI: You bet. I'll see you then.

(DR. BISCOTTI sees STEVE to the door, and STEVE exits. He then crosses to his desk, picks up his cell phone, and dials. STEVE re-enters the office, drinking water out of a Dixie cup.)

STEVE: What-cha-doing, Doc?

DR. BISCOTTI: *(A bit startled.)* Oh. I am making a phone call.

STEVE: To who?

DR. BISCOTTI: This is a private matter.

STEVE: You calling the police?

DR. BISCOTTI: *(He rises.)* We already discussed this now and I will see you tomorrow.

STEVE: I thought you said what I shared with you in here is just between us, that because of the law, you can't tell anyone else anything.

DR. BISCOTTI: Yes, what I told you is true.

STEVE: But it's not true about murder, is it?

DR. BISCOTTI: Actually, it is...

STEVE: *(Quickly interrupting.)* You should have said that, then. You should have told me that. You told me I was safe in here. Safe. Otherwise, how can I improve my life if I'm not safe?

DR. BISCOTTI: Well, you can improve it by not murdering anyone.

(DR. BISCOTTI hears someone on the other end of his cell phone answer, so he lifts the phone to his ear.)

STEVE: No, no. No.

(He breaks the boundaries by stepping from the far right platform onto the platform just to the right of DR. BISCOTTI.)

DR. BISCOTTI: Hello, yes, this is Dr. Charles—

STEVE: *(Reaching for the phone.)*

Give me the phone.

(He abruptly takes DR. BISCOTTI'S cell phone from him. This is the first time we have seen any physical contact.)

This is not supposed to happen. No.

(STEVE shuts off the phone and tosses it into the chair.)

DR. BISCOTTI: *(Trying to be calm.)*

I think our first plan is a good one—we take the night off to think about these things and try to calm down.

STEVE: I was calm. I was. I told you how I was feeling and that I was calm.

DR. BISCOTTI: Yes, but now it's my turn. For us to continue, I need time to do that—to get calm.

STEVE: But you said, Doc. You told me.

DR. BISCOTTI: It's time to go.

STEVE: This was supposed to be safe. I was supposed to be safe in here.

DR. BISCOTTI: *(Angrily.)* Your father was supposed to be safe. You should have thought of him. You should have thought about life, about taking someone's life.

(Beat.)

Now it's time for you to go.

(DR. BISCOTTI crosses to his door.)

STEVE: *(STEVE pulls out a gun that is tucked in the small of his back.)*

No. I'm not going.

ABBEY: *(ABBEY enters and steps up onto GEORGE'S old platform, which is far stage left. She is*

holding her painting and speaks to DR.
BISCOTTI as if he is out over the audience.)
I knew you hadn't replaced your twelve o'clock
client so I thought I'd stop back by real quick.

DR. BISCOTTI: *(Sensing ABBEY'S presence, knowing*
she's there.)
Steve, listen to me. You will not improve your life
by continuing to kill people. Please, put the gun
down. For you, do this. Put the gun down.

ABBEY: *(She turns the painting around, and it is*
beautiful, stunning.)
I sold it. Do you believe it? I sold the painting.
One-hundred dollars. Holy cow, that was fast.
Simple. I told them I had to quickly show it to
someone first, my mentor, and that I'd be right
back.
(STEVE remains frozen on DR. BISCOTTI with
the gun.)

DR. BISCOTTI: The gun, Steve. Put the gun down.

STEVE: No.

DR. BISCOTTI: Okay then, hand it to me.
(DR. BISCOTTI crosses toward STEVE.)

STEVE: If you try to take it from me, I'll shoot you.

DR. BISCOTTI: You don't leave me much choice.

STEVE: Choice? No, no, no.
(Sarcastically.)
You have choice, Doc. Lots of choices—you can
stay or you can go, but there are consequences
that go along with those choices. If you stay,
you'll get shot, and if you try to leave, you'll get
shot.

(DR. BISCOTTI tries to leave anyway, running for the door, and STEVE shoots him in the back, but for some reason, the gun doesn't go off. It doesn't work. DR. BISCOTTI is shocked but continues to run out the door. Breaking through yet another boundary, STEVE steps onto DR. BISCOTTI'S platform, center stage.)
NOOOOOOO!!! DON'T LEAVE ME!!!!!!!!!!!!!!!!!!!!!!!!!
(But DR. BISCOTTI is gone. Out of frustration and anger, STEVE turns the gun on ABBEY and fires. The lights on her platform go out. She falls to the ground. He then turns the gun on himself, shoots, his lights go out, and he falls to the ground.)

(When the lights come back up, we see a silhouette of DR. BISCOTTI sitting on the front edge of his desk, as in the beginning of the play, staring at his plate of biscotti.)

DR. BISCOTTI: *(Voice over.)* I suppose you wonder how I could have left my office, abandoning Abbey as I did. I'd like to more fully understand that myself. Self-preservation, perhaps? The human condition? I don't know. Had I stayed, I would have just added to the bloodshed; I know that *cognitively*. But it will be my plight in life to wonder, to go over and over these events again and again as I have here before you today—to think what else I could have done, how these walls, these boundaries, failed me, how will I be able to avoid the situation in the future? Can it be avoided—happenstance? I don't know. I don't think so.

(Pause.)

To question why it is I'm here—my purpose. Why didn't the gun go off when he tried to shoot me? And, of course, the question that plagues us all— how could God allow such things to happen, such random, senseless acts of cruelty to someone so beautiful... like Abbey? So, I can't help but think that maybe I should...well...that I should just get myself into another line of work.

(Beat.)

But then I remember Abbey's words, "Maybe there *is* some sort of dark force wandering around, trying to get us all to stumble." And maybe this dark force would like it, really like it, if I just...gave up.

(Lights fade to black as we hear the song "Maybe" by The Ink Spots.)

END OF PLAY

PERSONAL PROPERTIES

On Dr. Biscotti's desk are a soft directional desk lamp, a desk clock, an appointment book, a plate of biscotti, a glass jar of biscotti, two coffee cups, a classy coffee dispenser, and an appointment book.

DR. BISCOTTI: A cell phone in his pocket.
SHERIE: A purse with a checkbook, pen, and lipstick.
STEVE: Dixie cup of water and handgun with holster.
ABBEY: A purse, a beautiful original painting, and a
       Bible.

In the original Los Angeles production, the role of Steve was played by Paul Cuneo. (Photo by Steven L. Sears.)

Dr. Biscotti was played by Todd Covert.
(Photo by Steven L. Sears.)

Michelle DeLynn played the role of Sherie.
(Photo by Steven L. Sears.)

LISA SOLAND'S PLAYS

AN AFTERNOON WITH SHIRLEY and THE EMPTY
      CHAIR: Complementary One-Act Plays
CABO SAN LUCAS (Samuel French & Smith and Kraus)
THE CHRISTMAS TREE ANGEL RADIO DRAMA
COME TO THE GARDEN (Samuel French)
THE CORPORATE LADDER (Smith and Kraus)
DIFFERENT (Samuel French & Smith and Kraus)
DR. BISCOTTI & THE HUMAN CONDITION (All
      Original Play Publishing)
AN EARTHQUAKE (Dramatic Publishing)
THE FREEWHEELIN' BOB DYLAN (Quay Magazine)
THE HAND ON THE PLOUGH
HAPPY BIRTHDAY, BABY!
HOORAY FOR HOLLYWOOD (All Original Play
      Publishing)
IN THE UPPER ROOM (All Original Play Publishing)
INSPIRED! A Drama With Music
THE KIND THAT DOESN'T BUDGE (Samuel French &
      Quay Magazine)
KNOTS (Samuel French & Smith and Kraus)
THE LADDER IN THE ROOM (Applause Books)
THE LADDER PLAYS
THE MAN IN THE GRAY SUIT (Samuel French)
MATT & HIS CRAZY WRITING MACHINE (All Original
      Play Publishing)
MEET CUTE
THE NAME GAME (Samuel French)
THE OTHER SHOE (Smith and Kraus)
THE ReBIRTH (Applause Books)
REBOUND AND THE BATHTUB
RED ROSES (Samuel French & Applause Books)
THE SAME THING (Samuel French & Smith and Kraus)
SERGEANT YORK: THE PLAY (All Original Play
      Publishing)
SENSITIVITY (Samuel French)
THE SNIPER'S NEST
SPATIAL DISORIENTATION (Applause Books)
THREAD COUNT (Applause Books)
TRUTH BE TOLD (Samuel French & Quay Magazine)
WAITING (Samuel French, Smith and Kraus, & Applause
Books)

What they're saying about
SERGEANT YORK: THE PLAY

"It's simply a wonderful play."
– Deborah York, Executive Director of the Sergeant York Patriotic Foundation and great-granddaughter of Alvin York

"*Sergeant York: The Play* is... a powerful statement on the nature of war and the power of faith."
– Peter Colley, playwright/screenwriter/librettist

"I thoroughly recommend *Sergeant York: The Play* for any organization seeking an inspirational, wholesome tale of a true American hero."
– Burt Rosen, President and CEO of Knox Area Rescue Ministries Knoxville

"Soland has devoted her significant abilities to share the story of Alvin York's deep personal faith and commitment to Jesus Christ."
– Sam Polson, Lead Pastor of West Park Baptist Church

What they're saying about
30 SHORT PLAYS
FOR PASSIONATE ACTORS...

"Lisa Soland has here assembled a wonderful collection of short plays. If you're a passionate actor, a teacher or a director looking for a play to do, you won't find a better place to start looking than this book."
— Lawrence Harbison, Senior Editor, Smith and Kraus
& Applause Theatre & Cinema Books

"Lisa Soland's amazing collection of 30 excellent, sooo entertaining short plays is a must for any would-be playwright, actor or acting group!"
— *Tom Sawyer, novelist, playwright, screenwriter*

"This collection of plays is as varied and eclectic as the human mind itself. They are funny, dramatic, poignant, shocking, outrageous, satirical, imaginative... It's a must-have for writers of short plays and a great resource for theatres that produce them."
— *Peter Colley, playwright, screenwriter, librettist*